D1106479

Reflections at Walden

Walden Pond, Concord, Massachusetts.

Reflections at Walden

Selected Writings of

Henry David Thoreau

With a Biographical Essay

by Ralph Waldo Emerson

Edited by Peter Seymour

Photographs of Walden Pond

by Francis Rogers

and David E. Scherman

Hallmark Editions

CONTENTS

Henry David Thoreau (1817-1862)

HENRY DAVID THOREAU

by Ralph Waldo Emerson

HENRY DAVID THOREAU was the last male descendant of a French ancestor who came to this country from the Isle of Guernsey. His character exhibited occasional traits drawn from this blood in singular combination with a very strong Saxon genius.

He was born in Concord, Massachusetts, on the 12th of July, 1817. He was graduated at Harvard College in 1837, but without any literary distinction. After leaving the University, he joined his brother in teaching a private school, which he soon renounced. His father was a manufacturer of lead-pencils, and Henry applied himself for a time to this craft, believing he could make a better pencil than was then in use. After completing his experiments, he exhibited his work to chemists and artists in Boston, and having obtained their certificates to its excellence and to its equality with the best London manufacture, he returned home contented. His friends congratulated him that he had now opened his way to fortune. But he replied that he should never make another pencil. "Why should I? I would not do again what I have done once." He resumed his endless walks and miscellaneous studies, making every day some new acquaintance with nature, though as yet never speaking of zoology or botany, since, though very studious of natural facts, he was incurious of technical and textual science. He declined to give up his large ambition of knowledge and action for any narrow craft or profession, aiming at a much more comprehensive calling, the art of living well.

He was bred to no profession; he never married; he lived alone; he never went to church; he never voted; he refused to pay a tax to the State; he ate no flesh, he drank no wine, he never knew the use of tobacco; and, though a naturalist, he used neither trap nor gun. He chose, wisely, no doubt, for himself, to be the bachelor of thought and nature.

Hermit and stoic as he was, he threw himself heartily and childlike into the company of young people whom he loved, and whom he delighted to entertain, as he only could, with the varied and endless anecdotes of his experiences by field and river.

No truer American existed than Thoreau. His preference of his country and condition was genuine, and his aversation from English and European manners and tastes almost reached contempt. . . . But idealist as he was, standing for abolition of slavery, abolition of tariffs, almost for abolition of government, it is needless to say he found himself not only unrepresented in actual politics, but almost equally opposed to every class of reformers.

Mr. Thoreau was equipped with a most adapted and

serviceable body. He was of short stature, firmly built, of light complexion, with strong, serious blue eyes, and a grave aspect—his face covered in the late years with a becoming beard. His senses were acute, his frame well-knit and hardy, his hands strong and skillful in the use of tools.

Mr. Thoreau dedicated his genius with such entire love to the fields, hills, and waters of his native town, that he made them known and interesting to all reading Americans, and to people over the sea. . . . It was a pleasure and a privilege to walk with him. He knew the country like a fox or a bird, and passed through it as freely by paths of his own. He knew every track in the snow or on the ground, and what creatures had taken this path before him. One must submit abjectly to such a guide, and the reward was great. Under his arm he carried an old music-book to press plants; in his pocket, his diary and pencil, a spy-glass for birds, microscope, jack-knife and twine.

He loved nature so well, was so happy in her solitude, that he became very jealous of cities, and the sad work which their refinements and artifices made with man and his dwelling. . . . His soul was made for the noblest society; he had in a short life exhausted the capabilities of this world. Wherever there is knowledge, wherever there is virtue, wherever there is beauty, he will find a home.

'On the shore of Walden Pond. . . .'

from WALDEN, OR LIFE IN THE WOODS

In the spring of 1845 Thoreau began building a cabin by Walden Pond, about two miles from Concord, on property owned by Emerson. Thoreau moved in on July 4. His intention was "to live deliberately, to front only the essential facts of life," which he did for two years. Walden *describes how he lived and what he made out of the experience. The selections that follow have been condensed and rearranged.*

WHEN I wrote the following pages, or rather the bulk of them, I lived alone, in the woods, a mile from any neighbor, in a house which I had built myself, on the shore of Walden Pond, in Concord, Massachusetts, and earned my living by the labor of my hands only. I lived there two years and two months.

Some have asked what I got to eat; if I did not feel lonesome; if I was not afraid; and the like. I will therefore ask those of my readers who feel no particular interest in me to pardon me if I undertake to answer some of these questions in this book.

Near the end of March, 1845, I borrowed an axe and went down to the woods by Walden Pond, nearest to where I intended to build my house, and began to cut down some tall, arrowy white pines, still in their youth, for timber. It is difficult to begin without borrowing, but perhaps it is the most generous course thus to permit your fellow-men to have an interest in your enterprise. The owner of the axe, as he released his hold on it, said that it was the apple of his eye; but I returned it sharper than I received it. It was a pleasant hillside where I worked, covered with pine woods, through which I looked out on the pond, and a small open field in the woods where pines and hickories were springing up. The ice in the pond was not yet dissolved, though there were open spaces, and it was all dark-colored and saturated with water. They were pleasant spring days, in which the winter of man's discontent was thawing as well as the earth, and the life that had lain torpid began to stretch itself out.

At length, in the beginning of May, with the help of some of my acquaintances, rather to improve so good an occasion for neighborliness than from necessity, I set up the frame of my house.

Before winter I built a chimney, and shingled the sides of my house, which were already impervious to rain. I have thus a tight shingled and plastered house, ten feet wide by fifteen long, with a garret and a closet, a large window on each side, two trap-doors, one door at each end, and a brick fireplace opposite. The exact cost of my house, paying the usual price for such materials as I used, but not counting the work, all of which was done by myself, was: $28.12 1/2.

I give the details because very few are able to tell exactly what their houses cost, and fewer still, if any, the separate cost of the various materials which compose them:—

Boards	$8 03	1/2, mostly
Refuse shingles for roof and		shanty boards.
sides	4 00	
Laths	1 25	
Two second-hand windows		
with glass	2 43	
One thousand old brick	4 00	
Two casks of lime	2 40	That was high.
Hair	0 31	More than I needed.
Mantle-tree iron	0 15	
Nails	3 90	
Hinges and screws	0 14	
Latch	0 10	
Chalk	0 01	
Transportation	1 40	I carried a good part on my back.
	———	
In all	$28 12 1/2	

These are all the materials, excepting the timber, stones, and sand, which I claimed by squatter's right.

Before I finished my house, wishing to earn ten or twelve dollars by some honest and agreeable method, in order to meet my unusual expenses, I planted about two acres and a half of light and sandy soil near it chiefly with beans, but also a small part with potatoes, corn, peas, and turnips. My whole income from the farm was $8.71 1/2.

The next year, I did better still, and I learned that if one would live simply and eat only the crop which he raised, and raise no more than he ate, and not exchange it for an insufficient quantity of more luxurious and expensive things, he would need to cultivate only a few rods of ground, and that it would be cheaper to spade it up than to use oxen to plow it, and he could do all his necessary farm work as it were with his left hand at odd hours in the summer.

My furniture, part of which I made myself, consisted of a bed, a table, a desk, three chairs, a looking glass three inches in diameter, a pair of tongs and andirons, a kettle, a skillet, and a frying pan, a dipper, a washbowl, two knives and forks, three plates, one cup, one spoon, a jug for oil, a jug for molasses, and a japanned lamp. None is so poor that he need sit on a pumpkin. That is shiftlessness.

For more than five years I maintained myself thus solely by the labor of my hands, and I found that, by working about six weeks in a year, I could meet all the expenses of living. The whole of my winters, as well as most of my summers, I had free and clear for study. I have thoroughly tried schoolkeeping, and found that my expenses were in proportion, or rather out of proportion, to my income, for I was obliged to dress and train, not to say think and believe, accordingly, and I lost my time into the bargain. As I did not teach for the good of my fellow-men, but simply for a livelihood, this was a failure. I have tried trade; but I found that it would take ten years to get under way in that, and that then I should probably be on my way to the devil. I was actually afraid that I might by that time be doing what is called a good business.

When formerly I was looking about to see what I could do for a living, some sad experience in conformity to the wishes of friends being fresh in my mind to tax my ingenuity, I thought often and seriously of picking huckleberries; that surely I could do, and its small profits might suffice,—for my greatest skill has been to want but little,—so little capital it required, so little distraction from my wonted moods, I foolishly thought. While my acquaintances went unhesitatingly into trade or the professions, I contemplated this occupation as most like theirs; ranging the hills all summer to pick the berries which came in my way, and thereafter carelessly dispose of them.

When first I took up my abode in the woods, that is,

began to spend my nights as well as my days there, which, by accident, was on Independence Day, or the Fourth of July, 1845, my house was not finished for winter, but was merely a defence against the rain, without plastering or chimney, the walls being of rough, weather-stained boards, with wide chinks, which made it cool at night. I did not need to go out-doors to take the air, for the atmosphere within had lost none of its freshness.

It was not so much within-doors as behind a door where I sat, even in the rainiest weather. I found myself suddenly neighbor to the birds; not by having im-prisoned one, but having caged myself near them.

Every morning was a cheerful invitation to make my life of equal simplicity, and I may say innocence, with nature herself.

'The Essential Facts'

I went to the woods because I wished to live deliber-ately, to front only the essential facts of life, and see if I could not learn what it had to teach, and not, when I came to die, discover that I had not lived. I did not wish to live what was not life, living is so dear; nor did I wish to practice resignation, unless it was quite neces-sary. I wanted to live deep and suck out all the marrow of life, to live so sturdily and Spartan-like as to put to rout all that was not life, to cut a broad swath and shave close, to drive life into a corner, and reduce it to its lowest terms, and, if it proved to be mean, why then to get the whole and genuine meanness of it, and publish its meanness to the world; or if it were sublime, to know it by experience, and be able to give a true account of it in my next excursion.

Our life is frittered away by detail. An honest man has hardly need to count more than his ten fingers, or in extreme cases he may add his ten toes, and lump the rest. Simplicity, simplicity, simplicity! I say, let your affairs be as two or three, and not a hundred or a thousand.

Why should we live with such hurry and waste of life? We are determined to be starved before we are hungry. Men say that a stitch in time saves nine, and so we take a thousand stitches today to save nine tomorrow.

The mass of men lead lives of quiet desperation. What is called resignation is confirmed desperation. From the desperate city you go into the desperate country, and have to console yourself with the bravery of minks and muskrats. A stereotyped but unconscious despair is concealed even under what are called the games and amusements of mankind. There is no play in them, for this comes after work. But it is a characteristic of wisdom not to do desperate things.

'. . . the track is laid for us.'

Men esteem truth remote, in the outskirts of the system, behind the farthest star, before Adam and after the last man. In eternity there is indeed something true and sublime. But all these times and places and occasions are now and here. God himself culminates in the present moment, and will never be more divine in the lapse of all the ages. And we are enabled to apprehend at all what is sublime and noble only by the perpetual instilling and drenching of the reality that surrounds us. The universe constantly and obediently answers to our conceptions; whether we travel fast or slow, the track is laid for us. Let us spend our lives in conceiving them. The poet or the artist never yet had so fair and noble a design but some of his posterity at least could accomplish it.

I do not wish to be any more busy with my hands than is necessary. My head is hands and feet. I feel all my best faculties concentrated on it. My instinct tells me that my head is an organ for burrowing, as some creatures use their snout and forepaws, and with it I would mine and burrow my way through these hills. I think that the richest vein is somewhere hereabouts; so by the divining-rod and thin rising vapors I judge; and here I will begin mine.

With a little more deliberation in the choice of their pursuits, all men would perhaps become essentially students and observers, for certainly their nature and destiny are interesting to all alike. In accumulating property for ourselves or our posterity, in founding a family or a state, or acquiring fame even, we are mortal; but in dealing with truth we are immortal, and need fear no change nor accident.

'Necessaries of Life'

When we consider what, to use the words of the catechism, is the chief end of man, and what are the true necessaries and means of life, it appears as if man had deliberately chosen the common mode of living because they preferred it to any other. Yet they honestly think there is no choice left.

What everybody echoes or in silence passes by as true today may turn out to be a falsehood tomorrow, mere smoke of opinion, which some had trusted for a cloud that would sprinkle fertilizing rain on their fields. What old people say you cannot do, you try and find that you can.

Let us consider for a moment what most of the trouble and anxiety which I have referred to is about, and how much it is necessary that we be troubled, or at least careful. It would be some advantage to live a primitive and frontier life, though in the midst of an outward civilization, if only to learn what are the gross necessaries of life and what methods have been taken to obtain them.

The necessaries of life for man in this climate may, accurately enough, be distributed under the several heads of food, shelter, clothing, and fuel; for not till we have secured these are we prepared to entertain the true problems of life with freedom and a prospect of success.

None can be an impartial or wise observer of human life but from the vantage ground of what *we* should call voluntary poverty. To be a philosopher is not merely to have subtle thoughts, nor even to found a school, but so to love wisdom as to live, according to its dictates, a life of simplicity, independence, magnanimity, and trust. It is to solve some of the problems of life, not only theoretically, but practically.

If I should tell you how I have desired to spend my life in years past, it would probably surprise those of my readers who are somewhat acquainted with its actual history; it would certainly astonish those who know nothing about it. I will only hint at some of the enterprises which I have cherished.

In any weather, at any hour of the day or night, I have been anxious to improve the nick of time, and notch it on my stick too; to stand on the meeting of two eternities, the past and the future, which is precisely the present moment; to toe that line. You will pardon some obscurities, for there are more secrets in

'I never assisted the sun . . . in his rising.'

my trade than in most men's, and yet not voluntarily kept, but inseparable from its very nature. I would gladly tell all I know about it, and never paint "No Admittance" on my gate.

How many mornings, summer and winter, before yet any neighbor was stirring about his business, have I been about mine! I never assisted the sun materially in his rising, but, doubt not, it was of the last importance only to be present at it.

For many years I was self-appointed inspector of snow-storms and rain-storms, and did my duty faithfully; surveyor, if not of highways, then of forest paths and all across-lot routes, keeping them open, and ravines bridged and passable at all seasons, where the public heel had testified to their utility.

I have looked after the wild stock of the town, which gives a faithful herdsman a good deal of trouble by leaping fences; and I have had an eye to the unfrequented nooks and corners of the farm; though I did not always know whether Jonas or Solomon worked in a particular field today; that was none of my business. I have watered the red huckleberry, the sand cherry and the nettle tree, the red pine and the black ash, the white grape and the yellow violet, which might have withered else in dry seasons.

Finding that my fellow citizens were not likely to

offer me any room in the court house, or any curacy or living anywhere else, but I must shift for myself, I turned my face more exclusively than ever to the woods, where I was better known.

My purpose in going to Walden Pond was not to live cheaply nor to live dearly there, but to transact some private business with the fewest obstacles. As this business was to be entered without the usual capital, it may not be easy to conjecture where those means, that will still be indispensable to every such undertaking, were to be obtained.

As for clothing, to come at once to the practical part of the question, perhaps we are led oftener by the love of novelty, and a regard for the opinions of men, in procuring it, than by a true utility. I say, beware of all enterprises that require new clothes, and not rather a new wearer of clothes. Perhaps we should never procure a new suit until we feel like new men in the old, and that to retain it would be like keeping new wine in old bottles.

When I consider my neighbors, the farmers of Concord, who are at least as well off as the other classes, I find that for the most part they have been toiling twenty, thirty, or forty years, that they may become the real owners of their farms, which commonly they have inherited with encumbrances, or else bought with hired money—and we may regard one third of that toil as the cost of their houses—but commonly they have not paid for them yet. And when the farmer has got his house, he may not be the richer but the poorer for it, and it be the house that has got him.

Granted that the *majority* are able at last to either own or hire the modern house with all its improvements. While civilization has been improving our houses, it has not equally improved the men who are to inhabit them. It has created palaces, but it was not so easy to create noblemen and kings.

'Noble Villages of Men'

My residence was more favorable, not only to thought, but to serious reading, than a university; and though I was beyond the range of the ordinary circulating library, I had more than ever come within the influence of those books which circulate round the world, whose sentences were first written on bark, and are now merely copied from time to time on to linen paper.

Books are the treasured wealth of the world and the fit inheritance of generations and nations. Books, the oldest and the best, stand naturally and rightfully on the shelves of every cottage. They have no cause of their own to plead, but while they enlighten and sustain the reader his common sense will not refuse them.

How many a man has dated a new era in his life from the

24   '. . . undisturbed solitude and stillness.'

reading of a book! The book exists for us, perchance, which will explain our miracles and reveal new ones. The at present unutterable things we may find somewhere uttered. These same questions that disturb and puzzle and confound us have in their turn occurred to all the wise men; not one has been omitted; and each has answered them, according to his ability, by his words and his life. Moreover, with wisdom we shall learn liberality.

As the nobleman of cultivated taste surrounds himself with whatever conduces to his culture,—genius— learning — wit — books — paintings — statuary — music—philosophical instruments, and the like; so let the village do. That is the *uncommon* school we want. Instead of noblemen, let us have noble villages of men. If it is necessary, omit one bridge over the river, go round a little there, and throw one arch at least over the darker gulf of ignorance which surrounds us.

I did not read books the first summer; I hoed beans. Nay, I often did better than this. There were times when I could not afford to sacrifice the bloom of the present moment to any work, whether of head or hands. I love a broad margin to my life. Sometimes, in a summer morning, having taken my accustomed bath, I sat in my sunny doorstep from sunrise till noon, rapt in a revery, amidst the pines and hickories and sumachs, in undisturbed solitude and stillness, while the birds sang around or flitted noiseless through the house, until by the sun falling in at my west window, or the noise of some traveller's wagon on the distant highway, I was reminded of the lapse of time. I grew in those seasons like corn in the night, and they were far better than any work of the hands would have been.

I had this advantage, at least, in my mode of life, over those who were obliged to look abroad for amusement, to society and the theater, that my life itself was become my amusement and never ceased to be novel. It was a drama of many scenes and without an end.

'I Love the Wild'

Sometimes, on Sundays, I heard the bells, the Lincoln, Acton, Bedford, or Concord bell, when the wind was favorable, a faint, sweet, and, as it were, natural melody, worth importing into the wilderness.

At evening, the distant lowing of some cow in the horizon beyond the woods sounded sweet and melodious and at first I would mistake it for the voices of certain minstrels by whom I was sometimes serenaded.

Regularly at half-past seven, in one part of the summer, the whip-poor-wills chanted their vespers for half an hour, sitting on a stump by my door, or upon the ridge-pole of the house. When other birds are still, the screech owls take up the strain, like mourning women their ancient u-lu-lu. Wise midnight hags!

I was also serenaded by a hooting owl. I rejoice that there are owls. Let them do the idiotic and maniacal hooting for men. It is a sound admirably suited to swamps and twilight woods which no day illustrates, suggesting a vast and undeveloped nature which men have not recognized. They represent the stark twilight and unsatisfied thoughts which all have.

As I was paddling along the north shore one very calm October afternoon, for such days especially they settle on to the lakes, like the milkweed down, having looked in vain over the pond for a loon, suddenly one, sailing out from the shore toward the middle a few rods in front of me, set up his wild laugh and betrayed himself. I pursued with a paddle and he dived, but when he came up I was nearer than before. He dived again, but I miscalculated the direction he would take, and we were fifty rods apart when he came to the surface this time. It was surprising how quickly he made up his mind and put his resolve into execution. He led me at once to the widest part of the pond, and could not be driven from it. While he was thinking one thing in his brain, I was endeavoring to divine his thought in mine. It was a pretty game, played on the smooth surface of the pond, a man against a loon.

At length having come up fifty rods off, he uttered

28   'Walden wears best, the best preserves its purity.'

one of those prolonged howls, as if calling on the god of loons to aid him, and immediately there came a wind from the east and rippled the surface, and filled the whole air with misty rain, and I was impressed as if it were the prayer of the loon answered, and his god was angry with me; and so I left him disappeared far away on the tumultuous surface.

Once or twice, I found myself ranging the woods, like a half-starved hound, with a strange abandonment, seeking some kind of venison which I might devour, and no morsel could have been too savage for me. The wildest scenes had become unaccountably familiar. I found in myself, and still find, an instinct toward a higher, or, as it is named, spiritual life, as do most men, and another toward a primitive rank and savage one, and I reverence them both. I love the wild not less than the good. The wildness and adventure that are in fishing still recommend it to me. I like sometimes to take rank hold on life and spend my day more as animals do.

'Walden Wears Best'

This is a delicious evening, when the whole body is one sense, and imbibes delight through every pore. I go and come with a strange liberty in nature, a part of herself. There can be no very black melancholy to him who lives in the midst of nature and has his senses still.

Some of my pleasantest hours were during the long

rainstorms in the spring or fall, which confined me to the house for the afternoon as well as the forenoon, soothed by their ceaseless roar and pelting; when an early twilight ushered in a long evening in which many thoughts had time to take root and unfold themselves. In those driving northeast rains which tried the village houses so, when the maids stood ready with mop and pail in front entries to keep the deluge out, I sat behind my door in my little house, which was all entry, and thoroughly enjoyed its protection. In one heavy thunder-shower the lightning struck a large pitch pine across the pond, making a very conspicuous and perfectly regular spiral groove from top to bottom, an inch or more deep, and four or five inches wide, as you would groove a walking-stick. I passed it again the other day, and was struck with awe on looking up and beholding that mark, now more distinct than ever, where a terrific and resistless bolt came down out of the harmless sky eight years ago.

Men frequently say to me, "I should think you would feel lonesome down there, and want to be nearer to folks, rainy and snowy days and nights especially." I am tempted to reply to such,—This whole earth which we inhabit is but a point in space. How far apart, think you, dwell the two most distant inhabitants of yonder star? Why should I feel lonely? Is not our planet in the Milky Way?

I find it wholesome to be alone the greater part of the

time. To be in company, even with the best, is soon wearisome and dissipating. I love to be alone. I never found the companion that was so companionable as solitude. We are for the most part more lonely when we go abroad among men than when we stay in our chambers. A man thinking or working is always alone, let him be where he will. Solitude is not measured by the miles of space that intervene between a man and his fellows.

I think that I love society as much as most, and am ready enough to fasten myself like a bloodsucker for the time to any full-blooded man that comes my way. I am naturally no hermit, but might possibly sit out the sturdiest frequenter of the barroom, if my business called me thither. I had three chairs in my house; one for solitude, two for friendship, three for society. One inconvenience I sometimes experienced in so small a house, the difficulty of getting to a sufficient distance from my guest when we began to utter big thoughts in big words. You want room for your thoughts to get into sailing trim and run a course or two before they make their port.

In warm evening I frequently sat in my boat playing the flute, and saw the perch, which I seem to have charmed, hovering around me, and the moon travelling over the ribbed bottom, which was strewn with the wrecks of the forest. Formerly, I had come to this pond adventurously, from time to time, in dark summer nights, with a companion, and, making a fire close to the water's edge, which we thought attracted the fishes, we caught pouts with a bunch of worms strung on a thread, and when we had done, far into the night, threw the burning brands high into the air like skyrockets, which, coming down into the pond, were quenched with a loud hissing, and we were suddenly in total darkness.

Of all the characters I have known, perhaps Walden wears best, the best preserves its purity. Many men have been likened to it, but few deserve the honor. Though the woodchoppers have laid bare first this shore and then that, and the Irish have built their sties by it, and the railroad has infringed on its border, and the icemen have skimmed it once, it is itself unchanged; all the change is in me. It has not acquired one permanent wrinkle after all its ripples. It is perennially young.

Conclusion

I left the woods for as good a reason as I went there. Perhaps it seemed to me that I had several more lives to live, and could not spare any more time for that one. It is remarkable how easily and insensibly we fall into a particular route, and make a beaten track for ourselves. I had not lived there a week before my feet wore a path from my door to the pondside; and though it is five or six years since I trod it, it is still quite distinct.

I learned this at least, by my experiment; that if one advances confidently in the direction of his dreams, and endeavors to live the life which he has imagined, he will meet with a success unexpected in common hours. In proportion as he simplifies his life, the laws of the universe will appear less complex, and solitude will not be solitude, nor poverty poverty, nor weakness weakness. If you have built castles in the air, your work need not be lost; that is where they should be. Now put the foundations under them.

Why should we be in such desperate haste to succeed and in such desperate enterprises? If a man does not keep pace with his companions, perhaps it is because he hears a different drummer. Let him step to the music which he hears, however measured or far away. It is not important that he should mature as soon as an apple tree or an oak. Shall he turn his spring into summer? If the condition of things which we were made for is not yet, what were any reality which we can substitute? We will not be shipwrecked on a vain reality.

I do not say that John or Jonathan will realize all this; but such is the character of that morrow which mere lapse of time can never make to dawn. The light which puts out our eyes is darkness to us. Only that day dawns to which we are awake. There is more day to dawn. The sun is but a morning star.

from A WEEK ON THE CONCORD
AND MERRIMACK RIVERS

Of the river, Thoreau wrote: "At last I resolved to launch myself on its bosom and float whither it would bear me." Over a ten-year period he worked to expand the journal of the trip, making final editorial revisions at Walden Pond. The book was published in 1849, prior to the publication of Walden; *appreciative reviews followed, but few sales.*

SATURDAY: At length, on Saturday, the last day of August, 1839, we two, brothers and natives of Concord, weighed anchor in this river port. Our boat was in form like a fisherman's dory, fifteen feet long by three and a half in breadth at the widest part, painted green below, with a border of blue, with reference to the two elements in which it was to spend its existence. A warm, drizzling rain had obscured the morning, but at length the leaves and grass were dried, and it came out a mild afternoon. So with a vigorous shove we launched our boat from the bank, while the flags and bulrushes curtsied a God-speed, and dropped silently down the stream. Gradually the village murmur subsided, and we seemed to be embarked on the placid current of our dreams, floating from past to future as silently as one awakes to fresh morning or evening thoughts. We contemplated at our leisure the lapse of the river and of human life; and as that current, with its floating twigs and leaves, so did all things pass in review before us. There is, indeed, a tide in the affairs of men, as the poet says, and yet as things flow they circulate, and the ebb always balances the flow. All streams are but tributary to the ocean, which itself does not stream, and the shores are unchanged, but in longer periods than man can measure. Go where we will, we discover infinite changes in particulars only, not in generals.

When we had made about seven miles, we moored our boat on the west side of a little rising ground which in the spring forms an island in the river. The sun was setting on the one hand, while our eminence was contributing its shadow to the night on the other. When we had pitched our tent, we sat looking through its triangular door in the twilight at our lonely mast on the shore, hardly yet come to a standstill from the swaying of the stream; the first encroachment of commerce on this land. There was our port, our Ostia. That straight, geometrical line against the water and the sky stood for the last refinements of civilized life, and what of sublimity there is in history was there symbolized.

SUNDAY: In the morning the river and adjacent country were covered with a dense fog, through which the smoke of our fire curled up like a still subtiler mist; but before we had rowed many rods, the sun arose and the

'The wilderness is near . . . to every man.'

fog rapidly dispersed, leaving a slight steam only to curl along the surface of the water.

By noon we were let down into the Merrimack through the locks at Middlesex, just above Pawtucket Falls, by a serene and liberal-minded man, who came quietly from his book, though his duties, we supposed, did not require him to open the locks on Sundays. With him we had a just and equal encounter of the eyes, as between two honest men.

It is very rare that you meet with obstacles in this world which the humblest man has not faculties to surmount. It is true we may come to a perpendicular precipice, but we need not jump off, nor run our heads against it.

MONDAY: When the first light dawned on the earth, and the birds awoke, and the brave river was heard rippling confidently seaward, and the nimble early rising wind rustled the oak leaves about our tent, all men, having reinforced their bodies and their souls with sleep, and cast aside doubt and fear, were invited to unattempted adventures.

The wilderness is near as well as dear to every man. Even the oldest villages are indebted to the border of wild wood which surrounds them, more than to the gardens of men. There is something indescribably inspiriting and beautiful in the aspect of the forest skirting and occasionally jutting into the midst of new towns, which, like the sand-heaps of fresh fox-burrows, have sprung up in their midst. The very uprightness of the pines and maples asserts the ancient rectitude and vigor of nature. Our lives need the relief of such a background, where the pine flourishes and the jay still screams.

TUESDAY: Long before daylight we ranged abroad, hatchet in hand, in search of fuel. Then with our fire we burned up a portion of the loitering night.

We rowed for some hours between glistening banks trickling with water. Sometimes this purer and cooler water, bursting out from under a pine or a rock, was collected into a basin close to the edge of and level with the river. So near along life's stream are the fountains of innocence and youth making fertile its sandy margin; and the voyageur will do well to replenish his vessels often at these uncontaminated sources. As the evaporations of the river feed these unsuspected springs which filter through its banks, so, perchance our aspirations fall back again in springs on the margin of life's stream to refresh and purify it.

There were several canal-boats at Cromwell's Falls passing through the locks, for which we waited. In the forward part of one stood a brawny New Hampshire man, leaning on his pole. He inquired, just as we were passing out of earshot, if we had killed anything, and we shouted after him that we had shot a *buoy*, and could see him for a long while scratching his head in vain to know if he had heard aright.

WEDNESDAY: While we float here, far from that tributary stream on whose banks our friends and kindred dwell, our thoughts, like the stars, come out of their horizon still. After years of vain familiarity, some distant gesture or unconscious behavior, which we remember, speaks to us with more emphasis than the wisest or kindest words. We are sometimes made aware of a kindness long passed, and realize that there have been times when our friends' thoughts of us were of so pure and lofty a character that they passed over us like the winds of heaven unnoticed; when they treated us not as what we were, but as what we aspired to be. Friendship is evanescent in every man's experience, and remembered like heat lightning in past summers. Fair and flitting like a summer cloud—there is always some vapor in the air, no matter how long the drought.

We found a convenient harbor for our boat at the mouth of a small brook which emptied into the Merrimack. We sat on the bank eating our supper and we enjoyed so serene an evening as left nothing to describe. For the most part we think that there are few degrees of sublimity, and that the highest is but little higher than that which we now behold; but we are always deceived.

I dreamed this night of an event which had occurred long before. Dreams are the touchstones of our characters. We are scarcely less afflicted when we remember some unworthiness in our conduct in a dream, than if it had been actual. For in dreams we but act a part which must have been learned and rehearsed in our waking hours. Our truest life is when we are in dreams awake.

THURSDAY: The rain had pattered all night, and now the whole country wept. We managed to keep our thoughts dry, however, and only our clothes were wet. We no longer sailed or floated on the river, but trod the unyielding land like pilgrims. And we found that the frontiers had changed. Go where we will on the *surface* of things, men have been there before us. The frontiers are not east or west, north or south; but wherever a man *fronts* a fact. There is an unsettled wilderness between him and the setting sun, or, farther still, between him and IT. Let him build himself a log house with the bark on where he is, *fronting* IT, and wage there an Old French war for seven or seventy years, with Indians and Rangers, or whatever else may come between him and the reality, and save his scalp if he can.

FRIDAY: As the truest society approaches always nearer to solitude, so the most excellent speech finally falls into silence. Silence is audible to all men, at all times, and in all places. She is when we hear inwardly, sound when we hear outwardly. Creation has not displaced her, but is her visible framework and foil. All sounds are her servants, and purveyors, proclaiming not only that their mistress is, but is a rare mistress, and earnestly to be sought after. Silence is the universal refuge, the sequel to all dull discourses and all foolish acts, a balm to our every chagrin, as welcome after satiety as after disappointment. It were vain for me to endeavor to interpret the silence. She cannot be done into English.

We had made about fifty miles this day with sail and oar, and now, far in the evening, our boat was grating against the bulrushes of its native port, and its keel recognized the Concord mud, where some semblance of its outline was still preserved in the flattened flags which had scarce yet erected themselves since our departure; and we leaped gladly on shore, drawing it up and fastening it to the wild apple tree, whose stem still bore the mark which its chain had worn in the chafing of the spring freshets.

from THE JOURNAL

Throughout his adult life Thoreau kept an almost daily account of everything he saw, did and thought about. This was his Journal, *most of which has been published in fourteen volumes. The* Journal *ranges through Thoreau's life and philosophy, and offers many observations of natural life.*

I THINK that we are not commonly aware that man is our contemporary—that in this strange, outlandish world, so barren, so prosaic, fit not to live in but merely to pass through, that even here so divine a creature as man does actually live. Man, the crowning fact, the god we know. While the earth supports so rare an inhabitant, there is somewhat to cheer us. Who shall say that there is no God, if there is a *just* man?

The intellect of most men is barren. They neither fertilize nor are fertilized. It is the marriage of the soul with nature that makes the intellect fruitful, that gives birth to imagination.

Truly all men are not men of science. They dwell within an integument of prejudice thicker than the bark of the cork-tree, but it is valuable chiefly to stop bottles with. Tied to their buoyant prejudices, they keep themselves afloat when honest swimmers sink.

Men have circumnavigated this globe of land and water, but how few have sailed out of sight of common sense over the ocean of knowledge.

Perhaps what most moves us in winter is some reminiscence of far-off summer. For we are hunters pursuing the summer on snow-shoes and skates, all winter long. There is really but one season in our hearts.

Like cuttlefish we conceal ourselves, we darken the atmosphere in which we move; we are not transparent. I pine for one to whom I can speak my *first thoughts;* thoughts which represent me truly, which are no better and no worse than I; thoughts which have the bloom on them, which alone can be sacred or divine.

Almost any man knows how to earn money, but not one in a million knows how to spend it. If he had known so much as this, he would never have earned it.

I saw the reflections of the moon sliding down the watery concave like so many lustrous burnished coins poured from a bag with inexhaustible lavishness, and the lambent flames on the surface were much multiplied, seeming to slide along a few inches with each wave before they were extinguished.

Nature has looked uncommonly bare and dry to me for a day or two. I was therefore encouraged when, go-

44   *'. . . not to live in but merely to pass through.'*

ing through a field this evening, I was unexpectedly struck with the beauty of an apple tree. The perception of beauty is a moral test.

Many a man, when I tell him that I have been on to a mountain, asks if I took a glass with me. It was not to see a few particular objects, as if they were near at hand, as I had been accustomed to see them, that I ascended the mountain, but to see an infinite variety far and near in their relation to each other, thus reduced to a single picture. The facts of science in comparison with poetry, are wont to be as vulgar as looking from the mountain with a telescope.

Cultivate reverence. It is as if you were so much more respectable yourself. By the quality of a man's writing, by the elevation of its tone, you may measure his self-respect. How shall a man continue his culture after manhood?

I do not know where to find in any literature, whether ancient or modern, any adequate account of that nature with which I am acquainted. Mythology comes nearest to it of any.

What a faculty must that be which can paint the most barren landscape and humblest life in glorious colors! It is pure and invigorated senses reacting on a sound and strong imagination. Is not that the poet's case?

Do not tread on the heels of your experience. Be impressed without making a minute of it. Poetry puts an interval between the impression and the expression —waits till the seed germinates naturally.

A feeble writer and without genius must have what he thinks a great theme, which we are already interested in through the accounts of others, but a genius— a Shakespeare, for instance—would make the history of his parish more interesting than another's history of the world.

We believe that the possibility of the future far exceeds the accomplishment of the past. We review the past with the common sense, but we anticipate the future with transcendental senses. In our sanest moments we find ourselves naturally expecting or prepared for far greater changes than any which we have experienced within the period of distinct memory, only to be paralleled by experiences which are forgotten. Perchance there are revolutions which create an interval impassable to the memory.

My townsmen have been shooting and trapping musquash and mink. Am not I a trapper too, setting my traps in solitude, and baiting them as well as I know how, that I may catch life and light, that my intellectual part may taste some venison and be invigorated, that my nakedness may be clad in some wild, furry warmth?

Must be out-of-doors enough to get experience of wholesome reality, as a ballast to thought and sentiment. My thought is a part of the meaning of the world, and hence I use a part of the world as a symbol to express my thought.

Was awakened in the night to a strain of music dying away—passing travellers singing. My being was so expanded and infinitely and divinely related for a brief season that I saw how unexhausted, how almost wholly unimproved, was man's capacity for a divine life. When I remembered what a narrow and finite life I should anon awake to!

If a man has spent all his days about some business, by which he has merely got to be rich, as it is called, *i.e.*, has got much money, many houses and barns and woodlots, then his life has been a failure, I think; but if he has been trying to better his condition in a higher sense than this, has been trying to invent something, to be somebody—*i.e.*, to invent and get a patent for himself—so that all may see his originality, though he should never get above board—and great inventors, you know, commonly die poor—I shall think him comparatively successful.

from CIVIL DISOBEDIENCE

While living at Walden Pond, Thoreau was jailed for failing to pay his poll tax. From this experience came the following essay, first delivered as a lecture to the Concord Lyceum in 1848 and published the next year. It demonstrates Thoreau's immediate concern with slavery, which would soon lead the United States to civil war. More deeply, it expresses his profound and lifelong distrust of the civilization of his time—a distrust that led him to resolve "not to live in this restless, nervous, bustling, trivial Nineteenth Century, but stand or sit thoughtfully while it goes by." This essay has been one of the touchstones of dissent in our society.

I HEARTILY accept the motto—"That government is best which governs least;" and I should like to see it acted up to more rapidly and systematically. Carried out, it finally amounts to this, which also I believe—"That government is best which governs not at all;" and when men are prepared for it, that will be the kind of government which they will have. Government is at best but an expedient; but most governments are usually, and all governments are sometimes, inexpedient.

This American government—what is it but a tradition, though a recent one, endeavoring to transmit itself unimpaired to posterity, but each instant losing some of its integrity? It has not the vitality and force of a single living man; for a single man can bend it to his will. It is a sort of wooden gun to the people themselves; and, if ever they should use it in earnest as a real one against each other, it will surely split. But it is not the less necessary for this; for the people must have some complicated machinery or other, and hear its din, to satisfy that idea of government which they have. Governments show thus how successfully men can be imposed on, even impose on themselves, for their own advantage.

But to speak practically and as a citizen, unlike those who call themselves no-government men, I ask for, not at once no government, but *at once* a better government. Let every man make known what kind of government would command his respect and that will be one step toward obtaining it.

How does it become a man to behave toward this American government today? I answer that he cannot without disgrace be associated with it. I cannot for an instant recognize that political organization as *my* government which is the *slave's* government also.

All men recognize the right of revolution; that is, the right to refuse allegiance to and to resist the government, when its tyranny or its inefficiency are great and unendurable. But such was the case, they think, in the Revolution of '75. If one were to tell me that this was a bad government because it taxed certain foreign commodities brought to its ports, it is most probable that I should not make an ado about it, for I can do without them: all machines have their friction; and possibly this does enough good to counterbalance the evil. But when the friction comes to have its own machine, and oppression and robbery are organized, I say, let us not have such a machine any longer. In other words, when a sixth of the population of a nation which has undertaken to be the refuge of liberty are slaves, and a whole country is unjustly overrun and conquered by a foreign army, and subjected to military law, I think that it is not too soon for honest men to rebel and revolutionize. What makes this duty the more urgent is the fact, that the country so overrun is not our own, but ours is the invading army.*

Unjust laws exist; shall we be content to obey them, or shall we endeavor to amend them, and obey them until we have succeeded, or shall we transgress them at once? Men generally, under such a government as this, think that they ought to wait until they have persuaded the majority to alter them. They think that, if they should resist, the remedy would be worse than the evil. But it is the fault of the government itself that the remedy *is* worse than the evil. It makes it worse. Why is it not more apt to anticipate and provide for reform? Why does it not cherish its wise minority? Why does it cry and resist before it is hurt? Why does it not encourage its citizens to be on the alert to point out its faults, and *do* better than it would have them?

*Thoreau refers here to the Mexican War of 1846-48.

When I converse with the freest of my neighbors, I perceive that they cannot spare the protection of the existing government, and they dread the consequences of disobedience to it to their property and families. For my own part, I should not like to think that I ever rely on the protection of the state. But, if I deny the authority of the state when it presents its tax-bill, it will soon take and waste all my property, and so harass me and my children without end.

I have paid no poll-tax for six years. I was put into a jail once on this account, for one night; and, as I stood considering the walls of solid stone, two or three feet thick, the door of wood and iron, a foot thick, and the iron grating which strained the light, I could not help being struck with the foolishness of that institution which treated me as if I were mere flesh and blood and bones, to be locked up. I wondered that it should have concluded at length that this was the best use it could put me to, and had never thought to avail itself of my services in some way. I saw that, if there was a wall of stone between me and my townsmen, there was still a more difficult one to climb or break through, before they could get to be as free as I was. I did not for a moment feel confined, and the walls seemed a great waste of stone and mortar. I felt as if I alone of all my townsmen had paid my tax.

If others pay the tax which is demanded of me, from a sympathy with the state, they do but what they have already done in their own case, or rather they abet injustice to a greater extent than the state requires. If they pay a tax from a mistaken interest in the individual taxer, to save his going to jail, it is because they have not considered wisely how far they let their private feelings interfere with the public good.

The authority of government even such as I am willing to submit to—for I will cheerfully obey those who know and can do better than I, and in many things even those who neither know nor can do so well—is still an impure one: to be strictly just, it must have the sanction and consent of the governed. It can have no pure right over my person and property but what I concede to it. The progress from an absolute to a limited monarchy, from a limited monarchy to a democracy, is a progress toward a true respect for the individual. There will never be a really free and enlightened state, until the state comes to recognize the individual as a higher and independent power, from which all its own power and authority are derived, and treats him accordingly. I please myself with imagining a state at last which can afford to be just to all men, and to treat the individual with respect as a neighbor; which even would not think it inconsistent with its own repose, if a few were to live aloof from it, not meddling with it, nor embraced by it, who fulfilled all the duties of neighbors and fellowmen. A state which bore this kind of fruit, and suffered it to drop off as fast as it ripened, would prepare the way for a still more perfect and glorious state, which also I have imagined, but not yet anywhere seen.

Thoreau's early poetry first attracted Ralph Waldo Emerson's attention to the young man. Later, Emerson would decide that the verse did not live up to expectation, and Thoreau would rashly destroy all but his earliest works. The several early poems that survive are interesting records of a young man's initiation into nature.

Men Say They Know Many Things

Men say they know many things;
But lo! they have taken wings—
The arts and sciences,
And a thousand appliances;
The wind that blows
Is all that any body knows.

Sic Vita

I am a parcel of vain strivings tied
   By a chance bond together,
Dangling this way and that, their links
   Were made so loose and wide,
     Methinks,
   For milder weather.

A bunch of violets without their roots,
   And sorrel intermixed,
Encircled by a wisp of straw
   Once coiled about their shoots,
     The law
   By which I'm fixed.

A nosegay which Time clutched from out
   Those fair Elysian fields,
With weeds and broken stems, in haste,
   Doth make the rabble rout
     That waste
   The day he yields.

And here I bloom for a short hour unseen,
   Drinking my juices up,
With no root in the land
   To keep my branches green,
     But stand
   In a bare cup.

Some tender buds were left upon my stem
    In mimicry of life,
But ah! the children will not know
    Till time has withered them,
        The woe
    With which they're rife.

But now I see I was not plucked for naught,
    And after in life's vase
Of glass set while I might survive,
    But by a kind hand brought
        Alive
    To a strange place.

That stock thus thinned will soon redeem its hours,
    And by another year,
Such as God knows, with freer air,
    More fruits and fair flowers
        Will bear,
    While I droop here.

56   *'And here I bloom for a short hour unseen. . . .'*

My Prayer

Great God, I ask thee for no meaner pelf
Than that I may not disappoint myself;
That in my action I may soar as high
As I can now discern with this clear eye.

And next in value, which thy kindness lends,
That I may greatly disappoint my friends,
Howe'er they think or hope that it may be,
They may not dream how thou'st distinguished me.

That my weak hand may equal my firm faith,
And my life practice more than my tongue saith;
That my low conduct may not show,
Nor my relenting lines,
That I thy purpose did not know,
Or overrated thy designs.

The Respectable Folks

The respectable folks—
Where dwell they?
They whisper in the oaks,
And they sigh in the hay;
Summer and winter, night and day,
Out on the meadow, there dwell they.
They never die,
Nor snivel, nor cry,
Nor ask our pity
With a wet eye.
A sound estate they ever mend,
To every asker readily lend;
To the ocean wealth,
To the meadow health,
To Time his length,
To the rocks strength,
To the stars light,
To the weary night,
To the busy day,
To the idle play;
And so their good cheer never ends,
For all are their debtors, and all their friends.

The Railroad

What's the railroad to me?
I never go to see
Where it ends.
It fills a few hollows,
And makes banks for the swallows,
It sets the sand a-blowing,
And the blackberries a-growing.

1817 Born July 12, Concord, Mass.,
to John and Cynthia Thoreau.

1837 Graduation from Harvard College.
Taught school in Concord. Met Ralph
Waldo Emerson. Began *Journal*.

1838 Opened private school with brother
John. Trip to Maine.

1839 Trip with John on Concord and
Merrimack Rivers and into the White
Mountains, August 31 to September 13.

1841 Lived with the Emersons.

1845-47 Lived at Walden Pond.

1849 Published *A Week on the Concord
and Merrimack Rivers* and "Civil
Disobedience" (under title "Resistance
to Civil Government").

1854 Published *Walden*.

1859 Delivered speech "A Plea for John Brown."

1862 Died May 6 in Concord at age 44,
of tuberculosis.

Set in Linotype Aldus, a roman with old-face characteristics, designed by Hermann Zapf. Aldus was named for the 16th century Venetian printer Aldus Manutius.
Typography by Grant Dahlstrom, set at The Castle Press.
Printed on Hallmark Eggshell Book paper.

Designed by Harald Peter.